Fathoming my 3am thoughts

Deepanshi Srivastava

BookLeaf Publishing

India | USA | UK

Presentation by *BookLeaf Publishing*

Web: www.bookleafpub.com

E-mail: info@bookleafpub.com

ISBN:9789360945701

First edition 2024

To the ones who kept me warm in their arms,

My father who inspires me to become a better person everyday, my mother who opened the doors to the world of poetry and literature for me, my little loving sister, Shreyanshi who helps me keep going and my best friend who recognized the potential in me and motivated me in the darkest moments.

PREFACE

This book, or shall I say, 'A Place to Be,' is a collection of poems that I have written over the past few years, starting from the age of fourteen when I fell in love with the idea of capturing my moments in the form of poems. The idea behind sharing this meticulously curated collection with the readers is to make people feel that they aren't alone in any silent wars that they are fighting every day, the wars they don't usually talk about. Beyond mere self-expression, there's a deeper purpose to this collection. I want you to know that you're not alone. Life has a way of throwing hardships when we least expect them, leaving us battered and bruised. It's easy to feel lost in the chaos, to believe that things will never get better. So, whenever you find yourself struggling, I invite you to take a moment—a moment to pause, to breathe, and to find solace in these words. Make yourself home in your favorite place with a warm cup of coffee or tea in one hand and this book in the other. Let the verses wash over you like a gentle breeze, soothing your soul and reminding you that brighter days are ahead.

The last poem is a gift for you so make sure to read it but there's a condition, don't skip these pages!
Happy Reading, Fighter!

Table of Contents

Prisoner of Thoughts....................................1

"I'm okay"—your biggest lie.....................3

Tell me, Bon Vivant.............................. 6

That hollow biography............................. 8

We're everywhere................................. 10

Coffee beans and numbness......................... 12

Head above water................................. 14

My Youth without You..............................16

Replacements..................................... 18

The past... 20

My life in a suitcase.............................22

The ones who care too much are the ones left behind... 24

She understood it, all too well................... 26

Writer trapped inside a person.................... 28

Too bad at making decisions.......................30

No denials, no more............................... 32

The key to my kind of bar.........................34

Mirror - my critique............................. 36

Moments, not days.................................38

To feel and to overthink......................... 40

The final day.....................................41

Wrong Priorities..................................42

Morality and its cruel truth...................... 43

That thing.. 44

Loudness of the chaos............................. 46

Comforting lies - the medicines...... 47

Paper planes...... 48

Past 4 am...... 49

Who?...... 51

What happens if nobody's sane?...... 53

All my summers turned into rain...... 54

There's a new favorite body type in the town... 55

What was I born for...... 57

Transcripts of my heart...... 58

"You're too mature for your age"...... 59

Paint the canvas in beautiful shades of love.... 60

After you left...... 61

Her and them...... 62

Paradise...... 63

Souvenir for my ex-best friend...... 64

Labyrinth...... 66

Thirteen, fourteen, sixteen...... 67

Listen, listen to them all...... 69

Pure love - a cure for mortality...... 70

You and me - no longer in this universe...... 71

Ties...... 72

Scared to say 'hi'...... 75

Deja-vu...... 77

The next one is a gift...... 78

Dear reader, this one's for you...... 79

Prisoner of Thoughts

Free me, as I'm a prisoner of thoughts.
I'm a criminal under the section "Overthinking a
lot"
Right before things happen, I get anxious about
them.
I wouldn't say I have paranoia,
It's just that I pine for things to happen the right
way.
I've been in this cage for too long.
Often I find myself jeopardized by the sight of
people,
Who don't think as much as me.
They're happy, satiable.
Happiness comes to them so naturally.
It sometimes seems as though they are gifted,
with a reward of paradise dipped in merriness,
For not being cuffed in heavy and deep thinking.
I wish I could keep my anxiety aside for a
second
And be in the moment.
But as I am the way I am,
I end up falling into a labyrinth of regret.
I regret before, I regret after,
What is it like to not live like that?

Tell me, how does it feel like to walk under the
sun
And not worry when you'd get to feel the same
warmth again?
As I walk under the sunlight,
I feel as though I'm being chased by the
shadows of my past.
I have only my present to rely on,
Yet I somehow transpose my soul
into the heartbreaks that happened years ago.
Free me, as I'm a prisoner of thoughts
I'm a criminal under the section "Absorbing a
lot."

"I'm okay"—your biggest lie

How many times did you lie?
When somebody asked,
if you were fine.
You knew that you were breaking inside.
The bathroom walls
could hear you scream.
But instead, you decided
to put on a smile
and lie that you were fine.

Most days were clueless,
you couldn't get a hold of yourself.
You didn't have an idea
of what was going on,
you lied on the bathroom floor
talking to yourself.
You decided to take the blame,
you considered yourself the reason
for all the mess.
As soon as you heard footsteps,
you gathered yourself together;
wiping the tears that
you knew would come back.
That innocent smile in the vintage pictures,

those days when it was a sign of pure
happiness;
it has now become a way of
faking to others that you are fine and
not breaking apart everyday.

Nights get long
and sleep never came.
You made a thousand sacrifices
to God,
so as to catch sleep of a few hours
to function the next day.
As the sky changed hues every hour,
You woke up the next day.
Dark circles under the eyes,
the pillow was still wet
from your cries yesterday night.
You woke up pretending
that you were alive again,
hoping the new ray of sunshine
would bring something new,
Something more bearable than yesterday.
For a minute, you got happy,
for a minute, you forgot it all.

But then the pain swept in,
and here begins
the same day,
same cries, same pain.
Yes, the never-ending pain
and the lie, "I'm doing okay."

Tell me, Bon Vivant

Tell me, Bon Vivant
What brings you joy?
We're the same age,
yet we have two different worlds.
You smile most nights
that I spend crying.
While I'm made aware
of how terrible I am by others,
how do you manage
to get loved by all?
I try my best to be the
perfect version of myself,
yet you get admired for being yourself.
Sometimes I catch myself wondering,
if you saw a shooting star,
would a wish cross your mind?
For you have everything I want;
the happiness, the love in your life.
What one might think of you,
it surely doesn't affect you,
because you're busy staring at the stars
with the ones who love you,
without the fear of getting judged.
The truth is that I can't spend
one day in my life

where I can have fun,
without worrying
if there's a punishment reserved
for smiling too much.
I wish I could do all
the things you do.
If only I had a lucid life
where you hardly
had any clues.
So tell me, Bon Vivant
what brings you something
I direly want?
Which star did you see
a long time ago?
If you see a shooting star the next time
can you wish the same for me too?

That hollow biography

If they wrote my biography,
it would always be hollow and incomplete.
because they'd never know what it's like to be
me.
That sudden upsurge of emotions,
when you can't cry;
because the throat is heavy,
due to a thousand unspoken words
that have blocked the way through the chest.
How would they know what I feel
captured inside that one unforgettable moment?
Who'd give them that number
of times I've cried,
alone on the bathroom floor, all tired and my
heart bruised and battered?
For how many nights?
I don't think they'll be able
to fathom the chaos
that I feel in silence.
No one can gild
the wars I've fought inside of me.
Would they need the count of
tears I've wiped myself?
Surely not.
After all, it is more than a figure

that can be printed
as a number on a few pages.

9

We're everywhere - the things we own, the places we go, the people we meet

Do you want to know me?
I'll say no words,
no talks about my favorites or what I hate.
The things I own will
be the protagonists,
enough to highlight every detail.
That pillow on my bed,
it would give the number of
nights I've dumped
my face into it and cried.
The bathroom near my room,
its walls will echo
the words I've said out loud,
sitting on the floor,
with my head in my palms,
knees folded,
while trying to keep my calm and not lose
patience.
The half-used jar of coffee beans,
will tell a tale or two about the times
when I had to stay awake so as to
avoid the horrible dreams.

The sight of colorful book spines on my shelf,
they'd show how I find pieces of myself
among the thousand different books
that I read on Saturdays,
the nights when I stayed in.
That diary in the corner on table of my room,
the pages would tell how it was easier for me
to set my emotions loose on paper than
rant to the ones who might not understand
anything at all.

Coffee beans and numbness

I'm over-caffeinated again.
One thing's for sure is that it only happens
when I'm in pain.
My heart is so broken,
that my mind can barely think.
Even the most profound advice cannot hold me
from falling apart,
falling into no one's arms,
just alone again.
This wholesome world feels so lonely;
that is just so ironic.
Seven billion people,
and I still can't find the one
who's willing to hold me.
I'm sipping my coffee again,
just to stay awake,
because I don't want to see those dreams
that remind me of my loneliness.
I drink my coffee
like it's a goddamn mind-numbing,
gut-calming medicine.
I'll brew it till
the pain goes away,
so that my mind can start thinking rationally
and forget the labyrinth

it keeps getting caught in.
Friendship and love
are sometimes pure poisons,
because when they fall apart,
the heartbreak makes you go insane.
Here I am,
writing this while sipping a cup of coffee
over-caffeinated again.

Head above water

I feel distant.
I feel distant from the care I once felt.
All I can see is an ocean full of fears,
I'm alone by the shore,
of an undiscovered island.
All the love meant for me,
is on the other side of this bleak expanse.
None of it is visible,
just the sky and the fierce water,
coming after me.
It's not just one nightmare,
the ferocious waves have all that I hate,
it's coming to engulf me.
The sky is going to meet the waves,
the clouds are coming together
to hide the tiniest ray of hope
that I could possibly perceive.
It's all coming together to unravel my wrath.
I already sense myself drowning.
Where's the atmosphere?
Where's the air that I need?

Perhaps my loneliness is enough
to push it all away,
before I could put my head above water
and ask for help to last.

My Youth without You - a messed up timeframe

I feel like I lost my youth to you.
In an era where I should be making mistakes,
I'm instead observing this deeply,
digging for shadows of you in the people I meet
every day.
I stay constantly aware
in order to save myself from another one like
you
because I don't want to feel those dragging
emotions again.
I don't want to go down the same spiral.
I feel like an old soul so early,
tired of giving away my innocence,
again and again.
You took away my solitude.
You vandalized my innocence.
I wish I could take away all that I gave you.
I can't retrace enough and,
the silliest thing about
this whole hue and cry of us is that,
you did a bad thing which you don't regret.

While I did a good thing—trusting you,
and here I am remorseful, every single day.

17

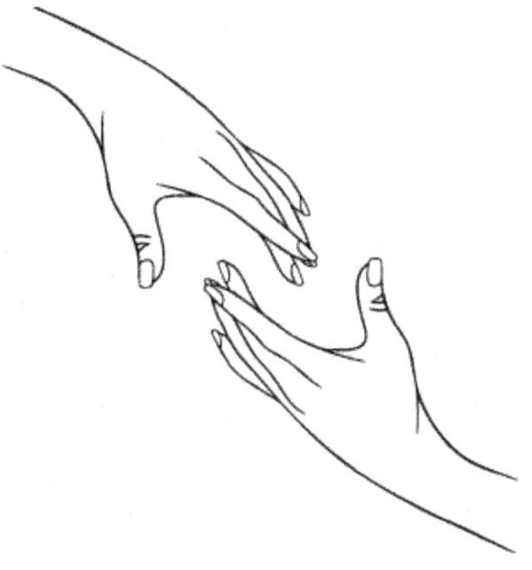

Replacements

Do you remember me?
Or have I been forgotten too soon?
Are those nicknames you gave me
still present at the back of your head?
Or do they now belong to someone new?
Did you delete all those texts that we
exchanged?
Are those GIFs still in motion?
Is my name still the same in your call log
or does that place now belong to someone else?
It's heartbreaking
how you are so pretentious
about us never being a thing at all.
As if I wasn't ever the person who
picked up all of your calls.
As if I wasn't the one who fought
at the frontier for you,
showed you your worth,
resurfaced your strength.
Still I'm the forgotten one.
Do you remember me?
We hardly talk anymore,
only when you need something.
I don't know how to ask how you are

because I'm scared you might not want to
answer.
I know I've been replaced by someone better.
They're listening to your problems now.
Do you still use the suggestions I gave you?
Are my pep talks still echoing?
Is that photo frame still on your shelf?
Are my letters kept somewhere safe?
Can you still recognize the pain in my voice?
Do you remember me or am I just a faint
memory at the back of your head?

The past

If my past were a lover,
It would be shrewd but primarily psycho,
chasing me around with the rotten flowers
that I forgot to water,
wearing a shirt inked in my mistakes.
No chocolates, no letters.
Just a few 'You never deserved me, anyway'
Be it the sunrise or the reign of the moon,
this lover won't ever leave my side.
The blame is still on something I did ten years
ago,
something I justified a long time before,
but my mistakes mean more than my intentions.
Never-ending arguments and one-sided beliefs.
It's just like a modern-day relationship,
like the paramours say,
'You're my end and my beginning.
I see you in every person I meet.'
My past visits me in different forms,
some days it's a person who doesn't love me
anymore,
while some days it's a brick of thought late at
night.

I wish I could break what ties us,
But don't humans find it hard to get over
someone?

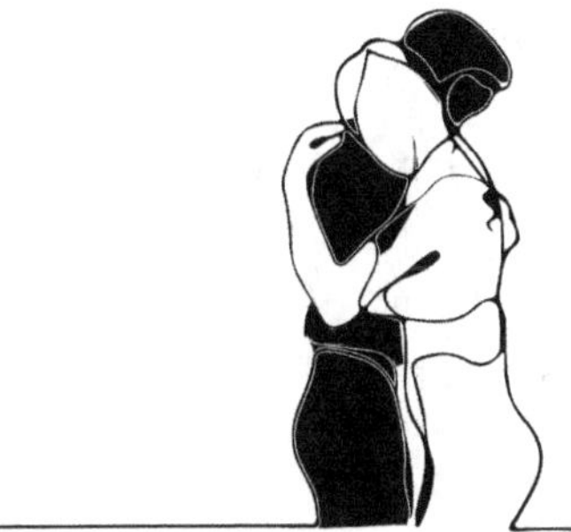

My life in a suitcase

The second I stepped outside my home
with my entire life packed in a suitcase,
I knew I would get lost in a world filled with people
who'd be constantly full of themselves.
I kept losing myself, piece by piece,
stranger after stranger who knew everything
about me.
I wonder what those twenty-year-olds have in mind
as they proceed
on a path they once described to be that of glory.
I've trusted, I've loved,
I've been betrayed, I've been thrown off guard,
by people who I thought would have my back
in a room full of double-faced back-stabbing
liars.
I see pictures and polaroids,
the captions beneath that say they found their
family.
Interestingly my archived section is filled with
faces
that I thought were a chosen bond over blood,
something that wasn't ever supposed to be
uncanny.

We were laughing, we were smiling,
we were looking at each other
as though the world was watching us shine
together as a whole.
As we walked those roads till 4 am,
promised each other a word or two;
those words are just frozen now,
just like our memory lane.
I get afraid every time I think of saying hi to
someone new.
I'm scared that
I will again be looked at as some temporary
substitute
for the ones who left them in this quest of
twenties and twenty-twos.

The ones who care too much
are the ones left behind

What is it that you got?
By believing the words of someone who never
took a sword
to defend you against the people who you
thought were yours.
I know all your stories,
your past, and how you've been running away
from it.
There isn't a single day that goes by
without you worrying that things would get
repeated.
We've had calls longer than the total time you
spent
with the people whom you chose over me
without giving it a single thought.
Were they the ones who held you when you
couldn't stop crying?
Why is it that the ones who care too much are
always the ones left behind?
I still find myself stuck inside a loop,
where I try to count the number of times I
messed up.

We grew together, we both made mistakes,
I thought we both knew that was okay.

She understood it, all too well

I still get goosebumps remembering
the words that would reach me
through hearsay.
The things you'd say behind my back
because you never wanted me to see
what was behind your pretty, perfect face.
You'd pretend you cared and said you'd be there,
but I still recall shaking and crying
and you stood beside me doing nothing.
"I'm kind of unemotional, I don't do well with
them."
I didn't take even a second to believe it
because at least you were being honest,
and wasn't that kind of true?
Those moments when I needed you
and thought you'd take a stand,
you used to stay silent
saying you didn't understand
little did I know
you understood it all too well;
behind that silence, there was a wish
a wish to see me fall and never stand.
I owe to fate for pulling us apart,
thank God I forgot your birthday
because I didn't want to keep making cards

for someone who'd treat them like logs of wood,
burn them to seek heat
since your heart was a little too cold.

Writer trapped inside a person

What should I do?
When I am a writer
captured in the body of a person
who's been trying too hard to meet the
expectations.
All that people pleasing,
making choices that I didn't like,
it all made me end up in a cage filled with
mirrors,
trying to make me reflect on the damage that I
did
when I chose to be someone
who was a mix of all the little things that the
world wanted.
Every day when I wake up, and I find there's
nothing new,
the same routine, the same scars,
trying to chase goals that won't lead me
to the place imprinted on my heart.
Sometimes, when I think about going back in
time
and changing the decisions that I took,
my heart says, "You will end up erasing all the
words

that are to be printed later in a book."
It's a labyrinth of thoughts if not an inescapable
maze.
The more I think, the more I feel,
the lesser the will to get out of that blanket.

Too bad at making decisions

Every night before I sleep and
let my thoughts flow over the papers of my
journal,
I can't help but see how bad I am at making good
decisions.
All these years, when it was in my hand
to make the final choice,
I ended up choosing something
that would later ruin the peace of my night.
Be it the people that I chose to keep close to my
heart,
or the path that I had to walk on
as an adult with teenage scars.
It's not like I'm not allowed to make mistakes,
but why is it that everything I choose has some
degree of danger to it?
It haunts me after and,
it haunts me later in the years.
Why didn't it haunt me before I made that
goddamn decision?
Is it that everything I touch turns into pure
poison?
Because the people around me are enjoying way
too much after making the same decisions.
Do I think a little too much?

Or do I calculate a lot?
Is it my perception that is misplaced?
Or is it my heart that's too scarred?
Whatever it is, I just want a few moments
when I can feel proud.

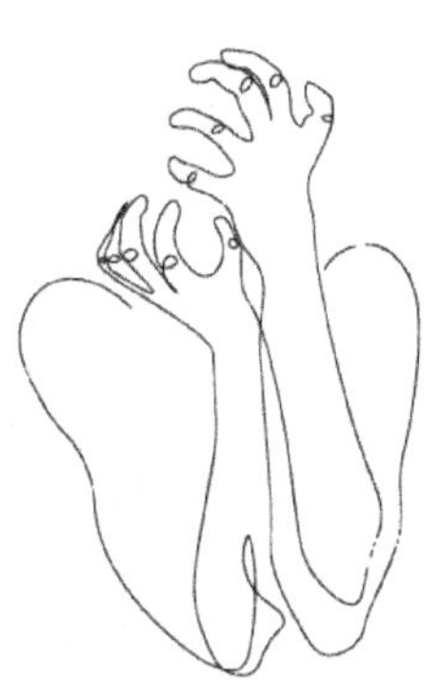

No denials, no more

How long has it been?
Since the last time you let your pain out.
Those tears,
trapped behind the strength that your eyes hold,
it's time that you let go of them,
and no longer suppress that stinging pain in your
heart.
Those who didn't treat you right,
look how freely they are moving around;
and here you are, a pure soul,
struggling to make it to the back of the yard
to get some fresh air and feel whole.
It's hard to let go and, it's tough to admit
that things aren't exactly going your way.
But how do we move on,
if we keep pretending that we're okay?
It's important to feel it,
may be all for once.
It's okay to have scars,
they'd heal as you move ahead towards the
future.

Let those thoughts go away for once,
Prioritize yourself,
It might turn out to be exactly the answer
That you've been looking for.

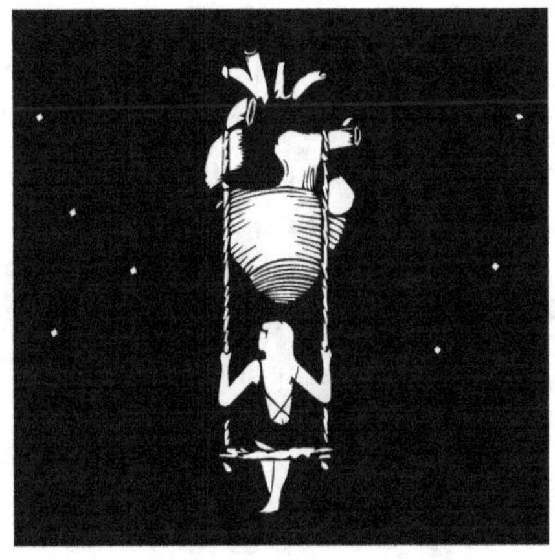

The key to my kind of bar

11 pm and they're still out;
wandering around with bottles in their hands,
hopping from one bar to another.
A room full of strangers
where no one can hear the other;
just people escaping their daily life
because sometimes it just becomes too hard to
handle.
I won't say I haven't ever thought about it,
the idea of a temporary relief.
But the means to get it hasn't been the same for
me.
There have been days
when the only time of peace started past 2 am.
My journal, my playlist
and the books that fit the idea of my parallel
universe.
I do want to go hopping just like the others
But I want to jump from one palace to another.
One palace is full of fragrances of the people I
love,
and the other one has the life-saving pages
that I unknowingly read out of boredom.
They need money to spend on something
that will make them spend more in the fifties.

The universes in my head need only a key
that the mind made out of distaste for the
normal.
Every night when it's so quiet,
my mind runs a marathon as if
it's supposed to reach a place before
Dawn seems to have appeared before my eyes.
I, too, love the idea of temporary escapes,
but what do I do
when it's the mind doing the work
and not my legs.

Mirror - my critique

Right from that time,
when I started looking into mirrors,
not just to merely look at myself
But to criticize and compare;
because enough wasn't ever enough.
One day I feel so sufficient,
and the other day
after going through my phone,
I feel that there's too much to work on.
One compliment and I'd be the prettiest girl,
half a sentence of the critique and
I'd fall thinking about putting on a mask and
being done.
I feel nostalgic for those times,
when the mirror couldn't talk
because these days it just has been telling me
to keep working out.
How do I look at my favorite bakery the same
way?
That comfort food has now become
a way for the insecurities to creep in.

Too many faces,
all caked with blushes and glitter.
How do I step out
without making my skin too clear?

Moments, not days

What are we afraid of,
when our heart knows life is finite?
It's those little glimpses from the past
that we often tend to remember,
aren't they such an escape?
When things fall apart in our lives,
Why do we want to take a step back?
Closing ourselves in a room,
letting our demons prevail.
Becoming vulnerable this often
only decreases the time left—
to celebrate.
The time that would have gone
into making memories,
is slowly slipping into vain.
When someone tries to shake your peace,
the power is in your hands—
to change the perspective of it.
Your happiness lies within your hands;
don't pass it over so easily.

Beating yourself up for that one thing not
achieved?
What about those little silent victories?
So what if they left you?

You were breathing before they came,
you'll get through this so beautifully.

To feel and to overthink

I wonder what's wrong with my head.
Why do I keep doing the same thing again?
At night, I always tell myself I won't let things
affect me,
but there comes the next day and
I see all of it happening yet again.
It's so hard not to keep falling into the same pit,
it's a habit developed over the years
to feel and to overthink.
It's mostly a curse,
But it gives me a way with words.
I don't know how I'll ever escape,
I don't see any loopholes.
My pillows, the bathroom, all know what I do,
I pour out the pain in neverending tears.

The final day

It doesn't matter what we are at the moment
unless it's the final day, which never comes.

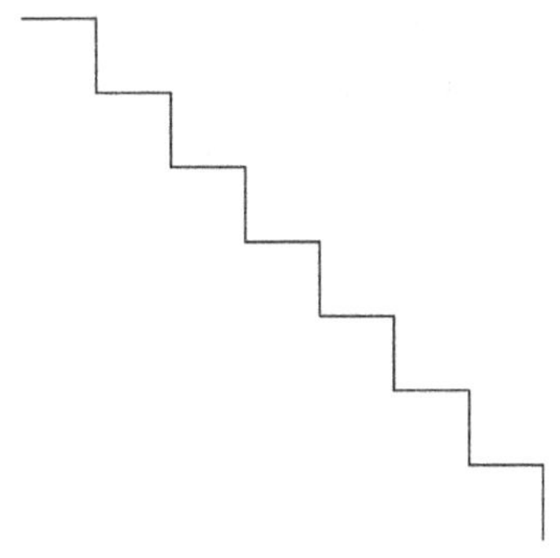

Wrong Priorities

Tell me why do we do this?
Prioritize the wrong ones
and push the right ones away.
I've been doing that for years
and I surely am tired of it.
yet I keep falling in the same pit again,
Is there really no one way to fix the perspective?

Morality and its cruel truth

I know someone who hates herself so much.
She loathes everything that life has to offer;
for she grew up in a selfish place where
everyone stuck around for a purpose and then
left.
Her family never cared about her,
she raised herself.
She learned the good by watching her people do
the worst.
Every time she heard the voices of yelling,
first things first in the morning,
she told herself she wouldn't do it when she
entered that phase.
She is tired of learning the harsh truths of life,
she wishes we lived without principles.
She wants those to be forever by her side,
those who were the reason for her not giving up
at her worst.
She knows about mortality and,
she hates its cruel truth.

That thing

Blank faces and liars,
wearing masks decorated to fake everything.
I am honest and not brutal
and god, I have to suffer because of it.
It often gets tiring seeing people get what I need
easily.
It's scary, it's cold;
every time I enter the arena, I get severely
bruised;
my heart gets so heavy,
and there develops that tightness in my chest;
years and years of trying to fit in.
It gets hard to detach from wanting
the fancy they created out of the ordinary.
I've dreamt of it before and I dreamt of it
yesterday.
Why do they make that one thing look so shiny?
That thing that I won't remember ten years down
the line,
that thing that I won't remember twenty years
down the line,
that thing is giving me the suffering
that I won't forget all my damn life.
It's scary and painful.
It's fancy and brutal.

I want to let go of it easily,
when it will be snatched away from my hands.
and I would be crying, my head between my
knees.

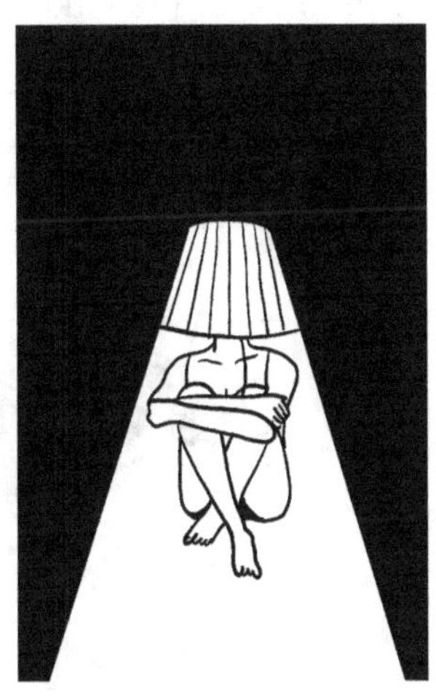

Loudness of the chaos

I'd rather bear the loudness of the chaos than the silence within the chaos with no clues around.

Comforting lies - the medicines

You're so beautiful,
yet I've to keep you so far out of my life.
The first day we met,
I wasn't even aware of how close
and far the distance between us would be with
time.
I met you thinking that we could never get this
close,
you left me thinking about
how could we ever get so far apart
in such a while
that was supposed to last my whole life.
I tell myself, 'I must be stuck in a bad dream.'
Comforting lies as if they are medicines.

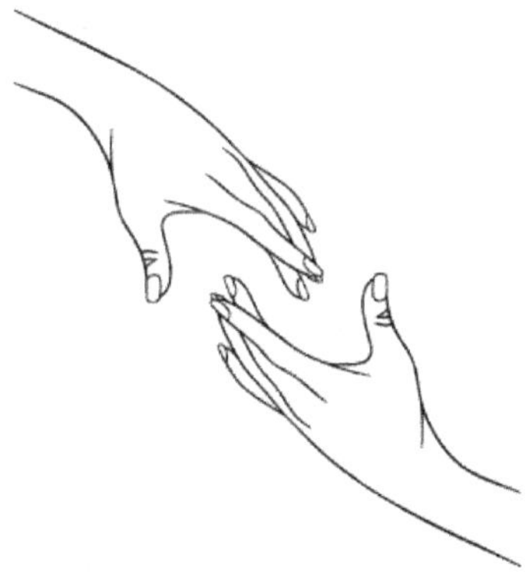

Paper planes

Dear paper planes, please bring me words of happiness and wisdom while flying high in the sky.

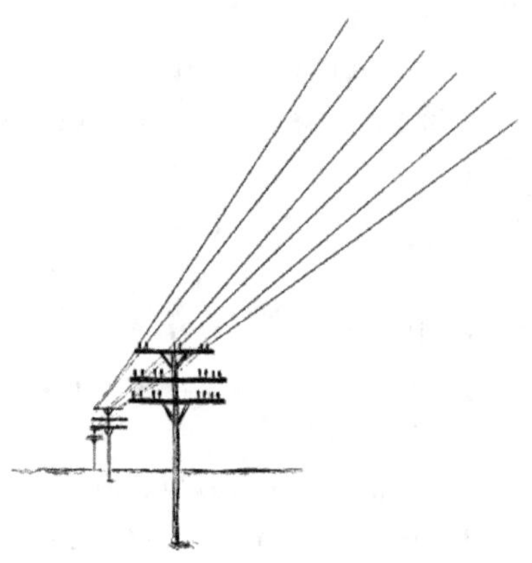

Past 4 am

It's past 4 am,
I'm still awake and
watching the screen of my phone.
face after face;
people's lives and how they have it all under
control.
It's going to be 7 am soon and
I'll have to start the day again.
New hatred, new jealousy, new goals
with that one song stuck at the back of my head.
Eye bags and disappointments,
that distaste for my so-called 'normal' life.
There is someone out there and sixteen,
cherishing things I will put on my vision board
when I am done with half of my out-of-control
life.
That girl with the perfect workout routine,
that boss girl having thirteen companies,
that girl with perfect scores and a perfect face,
when would I be 'that girl' who can find herself a
place?

It's 4:30 am,
I am still watching other people build their lives.
Soon it will be 5 am,
I will give myself the same comforting
lies—'One Day'

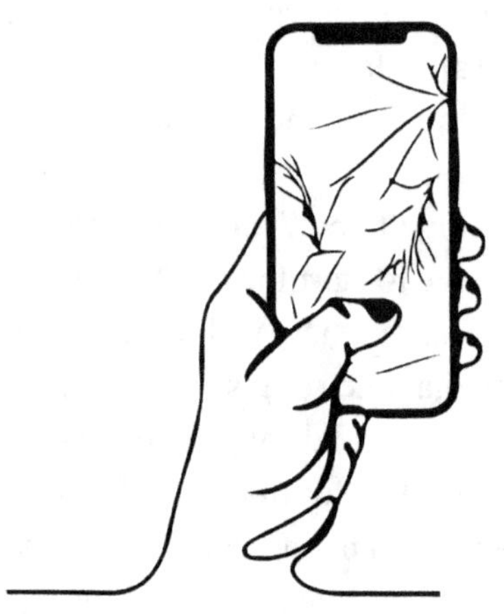

Who?

I'm stuck choosing between myself
and what they want.
Ever since I got a sense of things and this world,
there has been a constant war—
To live for myself or to be the person inside their
heads?
To breathe fearlessly and boldly or to be that
pretty submissive?
Every day I wake up with two pages in my
hands;
one leads me to the place with the path they
forged,
and the other one is simply the pieces of my
dreams
that speak of some beautiful alteration of a
neverland.
To be scared or to be bold?
To be selectively selfish or dynamically careful?

I wish I could figure out who it has always been
about—
impressing the world or
impressing the little child in me that they forgot
about?

What happens if nobody's sane?

That thin line between misery and denial, my sanity is the one holding it in place.

All my summers turned into rain

If I were to sit and recite all the different ways
things went south in the past,
it would take me an eternity to complete the
whole tale
and describe how it all continues to last.
That pain, those thoughts
that shake me to awakeness in the middle of a
slumber
that came after days,
those memories and what happened in the dark
after which all my summers turned into rain.

There's a new favorite body type in the town

Thirteen, and I wanted that perfect clear skin,
Fourteen, and I thought the curves weren't so
shaped,
Fifteen and, I knew for sure the glasses had to
go,
Sixteen left me thinking I lacked goals
Seventeen was a rock bottom for sure
because I started using apps,
compared myself with people all over the world.
Eighteen, and I thought—Is the skin tone that
great?
Nineteen, and I opened my closet,
thinking about what has to be replaced.

After being tired and shredded,
lost and confused,
the image of myself in my hands,
getting tossed around by the beautiful people,
I wondered if it all ever was worth it—molding
myself into different shapes
just to find there was a new favorite body type in
the town.

What was I born for

I hope I was born for something more,
something more than what this world hopes for.
Work, money, positions, and papers—I hope I
can create something that holds
eternal and immaterial value.
I hope I don't simply go away doing the normal.
I hope there's a place for me
where I can write my name and,
it would forever stay golden.
I don't want to be fifty and thinking—'I could
have dreamt more because now
I have limited memories.'
These days, I don't want to count
because I want to breathe every second
differently and make it paramount.
I hope I can write my destiny as I walk
down the path that I choose—something
different, something of my own.

Transcripts of my heart

If I could, I would
I would take transcripts of my heart
and print and highlight every line in different
hues.
The lines that talk about my pain would be hazy,
fast, and messy.
That page, from 'The Winter I Fell in Love,' will
be
cursive, clean, and pretty.
I'd frame the pages that would be messy,
blotted in heavy and dark ink,
probably from that night when I couldn't stop
crying.
Each page would be a different poem,
a different story to tell.

"You're too mature for your age"

Instead of being told I'm too mature for my age,
sometimes, I dream about what it would be like
to be too young for my age.
I don't want to be older than I am
because it's tiring and different.
I don't want to be called a girl with a special gift
who can understand things that they find bland.
Sometimes, I want to mess around and
not worry about what and what not the
consequences can
Can I get one day off and not be the mature kid
they need
so that there's at least someone who can
understand.

Paint the canvas in beautiful shades of love

your eyes, my universe
my heart, your canvas.

After you left

The nights have been lonesome and gray
since the time you left.
Nothing ever makes sense anymore,
To whom do I tell my secrets?
I can't bring together the pieces of myself,
that have been shattered, here and there.
I wish you could see what all fell apart
after you left.
Why were you around
when you never meant anything you said?
What's the point of wasting so much time?
You could have just spilled the facts.
You just kept building layers of lies,
one after another,
and I never wanted any of that.

Her and them

She was as fierce as fire,
They wanted to play it safe.
She was bold and wild,
They wanted a normal life.
She had new and different paths,
They wanted no risks and
forced forward the same old conventional ways.

Paradise

He's an art
and the artist.
Yet he reads my words
as if he hasn't ever created eternal masterpieces.
His words, golden
his work, a comforting paradise.
I wish he could look at the elixir his words are
through my eyes that behold respect and love
in the depth of the appreciation I hold
for the heaven he brought to earth
and gave me a taste of ecstasy.

Souvenir for my ex-best friend

Dear ex-best friend,
There's a souvenir I own,
that I think you should know about.
Last night, I opened the square wooden box
to take the letters out.
About fifteen were stacked together
on the top.
The paper had glitter and
a few vintage stickers that
you used to talk about.
The letters contained the words which
I wrote when I spent all my days with you.
They're undelivered,
I wish you could know
how they talk about
the happy moments I got to live with you.
A bit happy and a bit with the same ache in my
heart,
I kept aside all fifteen of them.
My eyes hovered over the few papers
that were hard and crisp due to my tears,
that the paper must have soaked
as my ink flowed on the paper,
jotting down about the pain

that I held in my heart after you left.
I held all those wafer-like papers and
kept them aside to reveal the final collection.
Something I had written close to the present
time.
There was one folded sheet left that I picked up.
Due to the suspicious looks of it,
I unfolded to see which emotion it held.
Turns out it was full of gratitude,
the thankfulness I felt.
for both your presence and your absence.

Labyrinth

I wonder what it feels like to live
without a fixed direction.
Maybe things aren't as rigid
and the heart can feel
a thousand different emotions.
It has been two years since I got stuck in this
cycle,
I just have been living the same days.
I want to run azure on a land without any fears,
I want to stand with my feet covered in sand.
All I want to hear is my favorite rhythm and the
ocean.
I don't want to eat, sleep, not feel and repeat.
I want to wake up to something different every
morning,
I want to lie down underneath the stars and
breathe.
It's tiring to keep living in this deep-seated
labyrinth.

Thirteen, fourteen, sixteen

My friends back home no longer recognize me.
They call me different names
because I got too caught up in understanding
life.
I have been twisting and turning,
trying to figure out my priorities;
while my twenties are thrown into my face
because I am slowly adulting.
It's my first time living life, and so is theirs.
I wish there could be some understanding.
How do I show them the 'behind the scenes'?
I tried talking
but my friends back home are no longer
interested in listening.
They called me 'selfish,'
called me 'crazy'.
I admit that I have been running too fast
to catch up with changes hurdling in.
I might have drowned once or twice
trying to balance my feet over waves
that aren't made for a novice.
I might as well admit that sometimes
it was all about me,
but my friends back home no longer remember
the time when

I made it all about them as there was a need.
I know I am changing,
I know that I am evolving as life proceeds
and the real world unveils its true self more.
I am slowly taking notes and adjusting,
but my friends back at home
no longer want to see the world through my
eyes.
They are caught in the childhood fantasy
while I grew up too fast.
because I left home when I was barely eighteen.
My friends back home no longer are with me
because I am twenty and they're still thirteen,
fourteen, sixteen.

Listen, listen to them all

oh, the art of listening
how beautiful it is.

Pure love - a cure for mortality

No matter how much you change yourself,
in the end,
you'll end up with that person
who will have nothing do with the color of your
eyes
or the curls in your hair.
Because eventually, we all find that person
who finds peace in our voice
and warmth in our touch,
paradise in our eyes,
and immortality between the lines and our
words.

You and me - no longer in this universe

I wish you were here
because there goes by no single day
when I don't miss you every passing moment.
Life isn't easy,
aren't we all aware of that?
But it was one hell of a ride,
when you were there.
You made me complete,
You made me feel okay.
Why did all of this have to happen?
I still fail to understand.
Today when I saw you,
I wanted to say hi.
I wanted to hug you so bad,
but then my reality told me
that we had already said goodbyes
that you aren't there anymore
that there isn't a 'you and me' in this universe.

Ties

There were times I remember
when I knew that I wasn't happy.
Still, I kept going,
believing I was surrounded
by the best people who knew me.
Even though I used to feel alone
when I was with them,
I did not mind it.
There were many times when I felt excluded
but my heart saw all those moments
when they cared about me.
I was diverted towards the positivity so much
that I could not see the overwhelming negativity.
Maybe I was insecure and scared to be alone,
That's why I continued to stay locked in between
the ties.
I accepted what they said without faltering
because I was scared that they would leave,
seeing that I did not know of perfection.
I changed myself over years and years,
So that I could keep fitting in well.
I kept losing myself
but that did not make sense at that moment.
I was so blinded by the ties
that I could barely feel myself.

When I looked in the mirror,
it wasn't my past self.
But I thought it was good,
After all, I was being liked by the people
who tied me in a world filled with lies.
Months kept changing, and so did I.
It was for no good;
and surprisingly, I didn't realize that.
Sadly, the time came which
I could never have imagined.
They let go of me
without saying goodbye.
When I rebelled to know the reason of the cause,
They silenced me like I never existed.
That night when I returned home,
I cried rivers that I couldn't swim through
with my head over water and
my feet touching the river bed.
What did I not change,
That they didn't like?
I stood in front of the mirror and stared at
myself,
It was not me who I was looking at.
It was the person they used to like.
I thought to myself, "All that for what?"
A voice whispered from inside,
"You were someone who you shouldn't have
lost."
Tiers come and go,

I shouldn't have let go of myself.
I was enough the way I was,
But I was too blinded to realize that.

Scared to say 'hi'

It hurts,
when I want to say hi
and meet new people.
I often stop my hand from moving,
because I get scared.
'What if they come and acquire
a place in my heart, again?
And when their hunger will be satisfied,
they'd decide to leave me,
without caring to explain.'
The cold truth about being abandoned
is not just the hurt that comes.
Every single time someone leaves,
you don't just hate them for doing so.
Instead, you hate yourself.
You blame yourself for being a terrible
company,
and for not giving all of yourself.
It hurts to be this vulnerable.
It's so hard to be human.

How can I just go and socialize?
When I am this scared of human attachments.

Deja-vu

It's 3 am,
I'm still awake.
It has been two hours since I texted good night,
I still haven't caught a wink yet.
My mind keeps catching random thoughts,
some from my past and some from my present.
The whole day I worked,
thinking I'd get tired and fall back.
The only escape I seemed to have
has now become a burden.
As the dark circles get deeper,
and my heart aches more,
I'm busy,
fathoming my 3 am thoughts.

The next one is a gift

Please know that,
you aren't alone.
Not today, not tomorrow.
Not ever.

Dear reader, this one's for you

Since you flipped the pages till the end,
you might have found pieces of yourself
here and there.
I know things have been hard,
especially the 3ams
that have seen you sleepless, tired, broken, and
unheard.
There might have been words that you came
across
which unlocked memories that you buried in the
past
The lines that you moved your fingers over,
they aren't so new.
They are little moments of my past,
captured in a word or two.
No matter where you are,
what you have been going through,
I know it will all get better,
you will see sunlight too.
Any day, anytime when something goes wrong,
come back to this book,
and make yourself home.

You aren't alone,
and so aren't your scars.